THE PROFITABLE WINE LIST

THREE STEPS TO QUICKLY & EASILY INCREASE WINE SALES

KIRSTEN HENRY FOX

CULINARY WINE INSTITUTE
Park City, Utah

Published in the United States by

Culinary Wine Institute, LLC
2100 Park Ave., #682594
Park City, UT 84068

The Profitable Wine List:
Three Steps to Quickly & Easily Increase Wine Sales

Library of Congress Control Number (LCCN): 2015935086

ISBN 978-0-9861576-0-8

Printed in the United States of America

Book cover design by: Deasy S. at eLance.com

Interior design by: Katie Mullaly

To Alyssa, Mitch and Hillary, my children, and Martin, my husband, for being the funniest, most supportive team any cork dork could possibly want.

CONTENTS

INTRODUCTION.. 1

STEP ONE - WINE LIST CREATION

Chapter 1 - STRATEGY................................7
How do I start a list?

Chapter 2 - SELECTION 11
How do I figure out the theme of my list?
Can I copy a list from a similar restaurant?
What size should my list be?
Should I select popular brands for the wine list?
Can I leave my wine list alone after I've got one?

Chapter 3 - SELLING WORDS 19
How detailed should I make my wine list?

Chapter 4 - PRICING................................. 21
How should I figure out what pricing will work?

Chapter 5 - PROOFING............................. 25
Does anyone really care about mistakes on my list?

STEP TWO - PRODUCT QUALITY

Chapter 6 - TEMPERATURE................................... 29
Does serving temperature really matter?

Chapter 7 - TOOLS..................................... 31
What kind of glasses should I provide?
What kind of wine keys should I recommend to staff?
What other tools will I need for proper wine service?

Chapter 8 - STORAGE 37
Where should I store our wines?
How do we store open bottles, particularly reds?
Should I consider pouring out of boxes?

STEP THREE - SERVER TRAINING

Chapter 9 - WHO 43
Should I trust my wine rep to conduct training?
Will my existing staff help new servers understand wine?
Should I charge my manager with training my staff?

Chapter 10 - WHAT.. 49
What does my team know?
Are there food and wine pairing mistakes to avoid?
What are the basics of proper wine service?
Is decanting really necessary?
How do servers deal with broken corks?

Chapter 11 - WHEN 61
When is the best time for training?

Chapter 12 - WHERE 63
Where should I hold my staff meetings?

Chapter 13 - WHY 65
Should my servers assist customers with wine choices?

Chapter 14 - HOW.. 69
Will a wine reference book help train servers?
How should my servers talk about wine?
Is there an example of an ideal server-training program?

CONCLUSION 75

ACKNOWLEDGEMENTS 77

ABOUT THE AUTHOR.................................... 80

Hi, Kirsten here... I know that as a restaurant owner or manager you feel like you have too much on your plate to read this 80-page book. I get it. Every one of my over-worked clients felt the same way, but many who've taken the time have enjoyed  a wine sales increase of 26%, 47% and even 119% very quickly. So if you have great intentions, but aren't sure on your follow-through, I've produced some free "cut-to-the-chase" resources for you here: *www.WineProfitPackage.com.*

―Kirsten

INTRODUCTION

As an executive sommelier, a sales rep for Southern Wine & Spirits, owner of a Fox School of Wine, and founder and CEO of Culinary Wine Institute, I spend almost as much time talking about wine and food each day as 15-year-old kids spend texting their friends.

For the most part, I work with amazing restaurateurs, people who are passionate about providing dining environments, wine lists, and menus that are scintillating and inspiring.

At a typical appointment with a restaurant owner or manager, I see a huge amount of interest in the wine list; the owner or manager really cares and wants to improve something about the wine program. I leave these meetings with a list of items to provide to the client restaurant and I am always very hopeful that the resources I provide will be useful to them – will help them either increase sales, or lower cost. Best of all, I hope I can help them gain footing in the often confusing world of wine choices and staff training. When I leave with my list of to-do's, I am invigorated because it appears that this restaurant will soon be on the way to more confident servers, happier customers, and higher profits.

I provide many different tools to restaurant managers and owners: I suggest new wines to replace those that aren't selling; I deliver wine tests designed to assess the team's wine knowledge; I create check-holder-sized cheat sheets for servers; I set up spreadsheets to help show mark-ups and how the wine list pricing should be updated.

And I follow up by phone. I follow up by email. I follow up by in-person visits.

But for the most part, nothing substantial changes.

Sometimes, I'm brought in to provide an hour-long wine tasting class. Sometimes, the wine list is updated. Sometimes the staff is tested. But it appears that once we've had our initial meeting, the owner or manager feels like they're on top of the program. No follow up needed. No systems put in place.

This is like meeting with a personal trainer once and then buying clothing one size smaller because you're sure the one-time consultation has ensured your weight loss success. Unfortunately, getting control of either your waist line or your wine list takes a little effort.

But once those systems are in place, just as with workouts at the gym, things get easier.

In my interactions with many, many restaurants, I've discovered a reliable, three-part approach that helps owners and managers take control of their wine program and I will share it with you in this book.

You're going to hear stories from the field. These stories are taken from real life restaurants. Of course, the names have been changed and, in an effort to remain concise, some of the stories are synopses of a few meetings instead of a meeting-by-meeting account.

After the stories, I provide guidance – useful, easy ways to squeeze more profit out of each bottle. I'm hoping that as this book gains steam, we will have a community of owners and managers who would like to share their stories of wins and challenges that may help others. (Join our ongoing conversation at *www.Facebook.com/TheProfitableWineList*.)

My goal in writing this book is to expose budding, new or even experienced restaurateurs to a clearer, easier way of thinking about their wine list, product quality and training. Through the tips and tools I provide I hope that servers will make more money, wine service at casual restaurants will improve, and margins will increase for owners so we will continue to have the luxury of visiting small, independent restaurants in our towns and cities.

This book is divided into three steps, presented in the chronological order to approach your wine program: 1) wine list creation; 2) wine product quality and delivery; and 3) server wine sales training.

I'm going to show you what has worked well for my client restaurants. One of the restaurateurs who took my advice has gained over 85% more sales just by changing the wine list contents and the pricing. Another has seen a 15% decrease in wine costs and a 13% increase in wine sales, for a net improvement of 28%. Yet another has seen an increase of 26% in wine sales.

Of course, I can't guarantee you'll get these results, but these stories, guidelines, and resources CAN help you if you're willing to shake things up a bit, if you really want to make money, if you back up your intentions with actions, and if you pour it like you mean it.

WINE LIST CREATION

STEP ONE

> *"The whole goal of serving wine in a restaurant is to demystify the process so the guests get what they want without feeling like they've been either randomly lucky or belittled."*
>
> PATRICK DELANEY, 25-YEAR INDUSTRY VETERAN AND DIRECTOR OF PHOENIX DIVISION OF SOUTHERN WINE & SPIRITS

"My biggest pet peeve is many restaurants that don't embrace wine service. Maybe they have a wine list, but no decent wine glasses to serve it in. Or a list that looks like they picked the wines out of a Kmart catalog, no inspiration in the selection and I am betting not many wine sales."

ALAN CHAMBERS, EXECUTIVE CHEF, SINCLAIR OIL COMPANIES

STRATEGY

CHAPTER ONE

HOW DO I START A LIST?

At our weekly meeting for Southern Wine & Spirits, we review the new liquor licensees in the area and then I visit the new restaurants in my territory.

One of those such restaurants was located in a stand-alone building, right next to a very busy road. It was packed with customers, especially given that lunchtime had passed. The restaurant offered burgers, steaks, a great kids' menu and other casual options. I met the bar manager, Tony, a cool guy with tats and a goatee, and asked about how I could help with wine suggestions, server training, etc.

Tony said they didn't have a wine list yet, and in fact, they had experienced guests leaving their tables when they found out that the restaurant didn't have one. He had gone to the liquor store and grabbed what was on sale so they could have something when someone asked.

"Glad you came around," he continued. "Not sure how we were going to figure out what should go on our list."

Wine lists are, at their very core, marketing tools for your restaurant. Just as menus, fliers, ads, signage, sandwich boards, and other marketing efforts can help show your restaurant in the proper light, your wine list can serve you and your customers by presenting your restaurant as you want it to be seen.

At the very least, having a list of wines available at your restaurant will satisfy customers who like to drink wine with their food. Having a nicely printed list allows your greeter or hostess to present the menu and wine list, giving the customers a moment to take in the atmosphere and the food and drink your restaurant offers.

As I start a new list, the basics I cover are as follows:

- What is the theme of the restaurant?
- Are there wines that, based on the theme, have to be included?
- Is a sparkling wine needed? (Terminology note: It is safest to refer to wine that has bubbles as "sparkling wine." "Champagne" is wine with bubbles that only comes from the Champagne region of France.)
- Are all the weight or body styles of wine covered? i.e., light-bodied white, medium-bodied white, and heavy-bodied white. Same with reds.
- Are there special foods or types of food that need special wines for pairing? For example, spicy foods require chilled whites, preferably slightly off-dry as the coolness and slight sweetness help alleviate the spicy burn.
- Is a dessert wine needed?
- How much storage does the restaurant have for whites, reds, and inventory?

If I am working with a restaurant that has a good amount of storage space, I suggest the following wines, at a minimum, to start their list:

- Sparkling wine – A Spanish Cava is a good starting sparkler because they are available for a reasonable price. Or there are some tasty, inexpensive Italian Proseccos on the market, as well.

- Light-bodied white – Pinot Grigio.

- Medium-bodied white – Sauvignon Blanc, often I recommend one from California, not New Zealand, because some people are not fond of the grassy/herbal aromas in Sauvignon Blanc from that region.

- Heavy-bodied white – California or Australian Chardonnay.

- Light-bodied red – Pinot Noir or Sangiovese/Chianti.

- Medium-bodied red – Merlot, Malbec or Zinfandel.

- Heavy-bodied red – Cabernet Sauvignon or Syrah/Shiraz.

- If you offer spicy foods of any kind, I would suggest an off-dry Riesling or a white blend.

- If your restaurant is located in a part of the country where people like sweet wines, I would have a White Zinfandel on the list.

- If you would like to offer a sweet, dessert wine, my suggestion is a Ruby or Tawny Port, as you can open a bottle of non-vintage Port and it will last months recorked in the refrigerator.

Following these basics, the theme of your restaurant should dictate other types of wine to include.

If you are not comfortable with starting your list alone, here are some resources for you to consider to get some help:

- Contact distributors in your area and ask for help.
- Ask one of your food or spirits reps to help you find someone in the wine industry.
- Do an online search for "sommeliers" or "wine educators" in your area.
- Use *www.LocalWineEvents.com* or *www.GuildofSommeliers.com* to search for a sommelier or educator.
- Call your local liquor store to ask if they have a consultant to help you.

The key is to partner with someone who understands what wines will pair well with your menu and what wines will sell. You know the food; let someone help you with the wine.

Given my experiences, if you just do this, you will be ahead of many of your competitors.

SELECTION

CHAPTER TWO

HOW DO I FIGURE OUT THE THEME OF MY LIST?

A restaurant called "Plates" offers small dishes from around the world: Spanish, Italian, Brazilian, etc. The food is interesting, delivering very-close-to-authentic tastes from great countries.

Their wine list? It consists almost exclusively of California and Washington whites and reds, mostly reds. They have California Cabernets and Chardonnays, Washington Merlots and Cabernets, and even a great array of California Paso Robles' Zinfandels.

Although the guests may be familiar with the wines on this list if they've traveled to wine country in California or Washington – or if they have heard of these wines from their friends – these wines are not going to show off the international dishes that the chef is preparing. A Spanish Paella goes best with a dry Spanish rosé or a Spanish Garnacha, not a bold, tannic Napa Cab.

Let's flip this around… You are in Umbria, Italy, and you find a nice, American steak house run by a couple from Sacramento, California. You are homesick and looking forward to a green salad with Ranch dressing, medium-rare Prime Rib, a loaded baked potato, and a nice, bold

Cabernet from California or, maybe Washington. On the wine list? Nebbiolos, Sangioveses, Barolos, even Nero d'Avolas. What a disappointment.

All this has to do with customer expectation. Just like a good restaurateur creates a menu with a theme, a well-written wine list is tied to the menu. According to Tim Taylor – my associate at Southern Wine & Spirits, and a 30-year-wine-industry veteran – a good rule of thumb is that at least 60% of your list should tie to the theme of your restaurant.

For example, if you offer small plates from around the world, 60% of your wines should be from non-domestic areas, preferably from the countries where your food recipes originate. If you open a Spanish tapas restaurant, 60% of the wines on your list should be from Spain. If you run an American steak house in Umbria, Italy, you should present some nice California Cabs or Washington Merlots to complement those dishes.

You can always save 40% of the list to offer more familiar brands and names.

Expectations set the tone for your guests' experience. You go to an ice cream shop for ice cream; you go to a funny movie to laugh; you head to a stadium on a Sunday to watch a football game. Your guests appreciate you taking the time to match your wine to your food, even if they haven't heard of the winery before.

CAN I COPY A LIST FROM A SIMILAR RESTAURANT?

I received a call from a restaurant owner, Vijay, for help with his wine list. He had a beautiful accent, which was unfortunate for me since I could only understand about every third word he said. After writing down what I guessed was his restaurant name, and making an appointment for, I thought, the following day, I searched online for his restaurant so I could prepare for the meeting. I found a full menu, and a full wine and beer list. I noted a few suggestions for the wine list and went to the restaurant the next day.

You can imagine my surprise when I pulled up for the appointment on time at a restaurant that didn't even have tables and chairs yet. The door was locked. I began to wonder if I had misinterpreted not only his restaurant name, but also the appointment time.

About 20 minutes later, Vijay showed up with his smiling chef, who spoke no English, to let me into the building. As we sat down, I commented on his existing wine list. "Oh, I copied that from a restaurant downtown. They serve similar food so I thought I'd just start with what they're doing. They've been open for many years." Turns out he'd called me to talk about server wine sales training, thinking his list was done.

Wine lists should be customized to each restaurant, just like menus are designed based on what the chef is skilled at producing for the customers in that area. A smarter tack for Vijay to take would have been to call a distributor or broker for help or visit the local liquor store and ask who in the area helps create wine lists.

Instead of a huge list of many different, eclectic wines that worked at the other restaurant's downtown location, I helped Vijay create a list that reflected the simpler tastes of the small townfolks who lived near his restaurant. The locals will be much happier when they come in for a get-together. We also redesigned the pricing to make it easier on the pocket books of his clientele. We made the wine list easy to read with short descriptions of the wines to help his customers feel empowered. THEN we talked wine sales training for his new hires.

WHAT SIZE SHOULD MY LIST BE?

I once walked into a new restaurant, a VERY casual, small pizza joint. TVs in the corners with car racing on one and indoor football on another. I picked up a copy of the wine list, which was printed on a piece of 8 ½ by 11 inch paper and had a few spots from food on it. It had 24 wines by the glass, only by the glass, and I was familiar with most of the wines, some of which topped $40 per bottle at the liquor store. I asked to see the manager or owner. Jackie comes around the corner, with a cell phone to her ear, waving at me to sit down at a table.

"Oh, I don't drink wine," she explains, checking her email while she talks to me. "I just bought this place and wanted to put something on the menu, so I went to the liquor store, bought a variety of wines and put them all on my list. I figure I'll see what sells and then only keep those."

I asked her how many glasses of wine she was selling on an average night. "Two, maybe four. Our beer is much more popular." How much spoiled wine was she pouring down the drain? "Oh I don't really keep track of that."

She was out of business in six months.

Start small. This is the most basic list I use. You can always add new products as you dial in what your customers want.

- One sparkling by the bottle.
- One light white by the glass and bottle.
- One heavy white by the glass and bottle.
- One light red by the glass and bottle.
- One heavy red by the glass and bottle.
- One off-dry white or pink by the glass and bottle.

If you are willing to add a few more options, start with upsell options for each of the categories above. Then, depending on the theme of your restaurant, add appropriate types of wine that come from the same regions as your food. For example, Northern Italian restaurants should be offering some Northern Italian wines from Piedmont and the Veneto.

If you want a 30-40 item list, I've set up a spreadsheet that you can use to help figure out what types of wines to select. Go to *www.WineProfitPackage.com*.

Before you end up pouring lots of wine that's turned to vinegar down the drain, give yourself a simple start on your list so the open bottles are limited and you are moving through them quickly.

SHOULD I SELECT POPULAR BRANDS FOR THE WINE LIST?

It was lightly snowing out, about two weeks before Christmas, as I walked into one newish restaurant. The owner, Sarah, was having a bad day. She had just returned from the liquor store.

"And, let me tell you, I'm from Miami. I still don't know how to drive in the snow. Jeez..." she railed. Her hair was wet, and she returned with only three of the eleven wines on her list. The other eight were on special Christmas deals and were out of stock because, she vented, "They were swooped up by yahoos for their parties."

Her wine list was useless and she was heading into the busiest time of the year.

Wines that do well in sales to consumers aren't always the best fit for wine lists. It is not a problem to include a couple, but creating a list exclusively offering these "grocery store brands" will not convey a sense of originality to your guests. This is somewhat akin to buying pies from Marie Callender's® and selling them at your restaurant. You may get a few takers who are happy you have something they recognize, but you will be missing the many patrons who enjoy the experience of unique offerings.

The other challenge with popular consumer wines is that you may have trouble finding them at key times, like Sarah. Supplies may run low both with retailers and distributors.

Rather than focusing on actual brands of wines that are popular, watch what TYPES of wine are selling. Look for trends. Once you have established what types of wine are selling and you have looked into which wine will work with your food, you can look at price ranges and select non-grocery-store-brand options that fit for your specific restaurant.

And sure, you can put some big brands on your list, just make sure they're not the only ones on it.

CAN I LEAVE MY WINE LIST ALONE AFTER I'VE GOT ONE?

I was at one mid-level restaurant, working with the bar manager, Dave – a super nice guy, hard worker and devoted to making the restaurant a better place. Dave had some great ideas about the list and, over the course of many meetings, we perfected a new mix of wines, weeded out the duds, and created a better pricing pattern. We eliminated five Sherries by the glass, for example, not one of which had sold in six months.

I went in to see Dave a month or so later to find out how the new list was working. The extremely cautious owner of the restaurant had stepped in. He told Dave that he could change anything he wanted on the wine list, as long as there was not one complaint from a customer. If there was a complaint about a missing wine or a more expensive price, Dave would be called in to speak for his decisions.

So, as you can imagine, the list remained the same.

For non-wine people like the owner of this restaurant, wine is wine. But if you pay attention, there are trends in wine. One, formally non-popular wine varietal becomes popular seemingly overnight. Another previously hot seller starts moving down your list of re-orders needed.

At a minimum, once a year you should be changing up your list, but I highly recommend doing this twice a year, so each version will pair best with your winter and summer food menus. For one cranky customer who notices that a price may have jumped $0.25, you'll have five looking the wine list over to find new options.

If you are too busy to watch wine, find someone to watch it for you: a wine broker, an interested server, a wine store employee. Ask questions of someone in the industry. They are watching hot trends all the time.

If you've left your list alone for a long time, you may get some push-back from your regulars as they see the changes for the first time – but steel yourself, and tell your guests you are making an effort to stay fresh and current for them. Just like you update your food menu, you're now updating your wine list.

If you don't, your list is slowly becoming a liability; your guests won't see what they're looking for and you won't be making the money you should be.

SELLING WORDS

CHAPTER THREE

HOW DETAILED SHOULD I MAKE MY WINE LIST?

I was at a restaurant that had one of the most extensive Italian wine lists I'd seen, a list subdivided by regions in Italy: "Umbria," "Veneto," "Sardinia." The list had at least 100 wines complete with name, vintage, wine area and price. I loved the breadth of what they offered. I began analyzing which dish I would order in combination with which wine… Cool or warm region? Piedmont or Puglia? Trentino-Alto Adige or Campania? My poor dining partner, Mitch, had plenty of time to check his Facebook feed because for a time, I talked to him only in regards to what his menu choice was so I could find the perfect wine for us to share. Which wine… which wine… I was in heaven… but no one knew my background at that restaurant and no one offered to help me.

I'm an executive sommelier and a certified wine specialist; I belong to the Society of Wine Educators and the Guild of Sommeliers. I study wine every day. I sell wine to restaurants, and I write wine lists.

Unless your staff is very, very well trained in selling wine or your guests are all total, complete wine geeks like me, you've lost them at "Hello, here is our wine list" as the heavy book is pressed into their hands. What does the heading "Puglia" mean to most people? You risk them being too intimidated to ask questions, or worse, humiliated because they don't understand. Intimidated, humiliated customers aren't likely to order wine or to think of your establishment next time around. Not good for repeat business.

Organize your list in the way that makes the most sense to you. However, assuming you don't have a sommelier on staff to help guests, note a few characteristics that average people understand as a reference point. For example, I like to see three descriptors at a minimum for each wine: 1) weight or body style of the wine, 2) a key fruit seen in the wine and, 3) a selling word. For example in the story above: for Pinot Grigio, "light-bodied, citrusy, crisp"; or for Primativo, "medium-weight, black fruit, jammy."

Depending on the familiarity of the wines you're offering to the average American, you may even consider making suggestions on each of your menu items as to a red and a white from your wine list that pair with the dish.

You probably have your menu items described to set expectations and describe your foods. Your wines should be given the same love.

PRICING

CHAPTER FOUR

HOW SHOULD I FIGURE OUT WHAT PRICING WILL WORK?

I went into one restaurant, located in a small hotel in a suburb, which offered a casual steakhouse menu with some very tasty cuts of meat. When I looked at their wine list, I almost dropped it. Nothing on their list was under $45, and the wines they were listing for $45 were available for sale at the liquor store for $11.

When I sat down with the 40ish, athletic-looking manager, Kathleen, I asked about the list pricing.

"The owners are real sticklers about that," she said. "We've had complaints but they won't budge on their pricing. They say that pricing the wines high helps define us as a nice restaurant."

"How are the wines selling?" I asked.

"We sell a few of the really expensive ones," she explained, "but not as many bottles overall as I would expect in a restaurant of this size."

People are not stupid, especially when it comes to spending their money. If you are not a fine-dining establishment and you have priced your wines four times the cost of the local liquor store pricing, they will not buy your wine… or not much of it.

You need to price the wines for your location and the market you are trying to satisfy at a reasonable markup.

Start with figuring out your wine list's sweet spot. Since I'm sure you've spent time figuring out how to price your menu – taking into account your area, competitors, theme of your restaurant, etc. – look at your average entrée price and then double it, that will give you your wine list sweet spot. For example, if your average entrée is $17 per person, your wine list sweet spot is $34. One third of the bottles should be priced lower than $34. About one third of the bottles can be in the $34 range, and one third of the bottles should be priced more highly.

This allows for both downsell and upsell depending on what your customers want.

ANOTHER PERSPECTIVE ON PRICING:

Another of the steakhouse restaurants I helped wasn't selling much of any wine on their list. I met with the manager, Meghan, who was giving her life and blood to this restaurant. Her mascara was a little smudged and her hair was a bit tousled, but her smile was genuine. She really loved this place. She actually had a cot in her office since she was spending so many hours there.

I looked at their wine list. Their mix of wines wasn't the problem; they had the primary varietals that you'd expect at an American steakhouse, along with some interesting additions. You could easily read the names of the wines and the wine appellations, so the type face was clear and big enough. I told her I would work on this back at my office.

After throwing their list of wines into my handy-dandy spreadsheet, (See www.WineProfitPackage.com to download a free copy), the problem became clear: their pricing was all over the place. They had a $26 bottle of wine marked up to $36 and a $22 bottle on the list at $45. They had an $11 Sauvignon Blanc for $10 a glass and $45 a bottle. They had a $35 Rioja red for $9 a glass and $45 a bottle on the list.

This was so random that, if I was the customer, I would begin to feel taken advantage of, so rather than try to figure out the best deal, I would avoid ordering wine. And then, in light of the wine list, I'd begin to wonder whether the dish I was ordering was ridiculously marked up, or a smokin' deal. Am I a sucker or a value finder? With this kind of angst, you can bet that I would be looking for a different location my next time out.

I agree with Michael Szczesny, Level Two Sommelier and wine rep for Young's Market Mountain States Division, who says that if a restaurant really wants to sell wine, they should use tiers of mark-up: high, medium, low, and super low.

- Low priced wines get a higher mark up.
- Sweet-spot wines get a medium mark up for your area and market.
- High-priced wines get a lower mark up.
- Super high-end wines get a very low mark up.

How can you make money with this system? First, the wines in the least expensive tier will sell because wine drinkers will always order something. Your sweet spot wines (sweet spot = double your average entrée) will sell because a table of two sees them as the perfect solution.

In regards to your super high-priced wines if you choose to carry some, Szczesny continues, "If you use a 2.0 mark up, you would take an $80 bottle of wine and it would end up $160 per bottle on your list. Let's say you sell two bottles of this expensive wine. You'll be making 2 x $80 profit = $160."

The more profitable way? "If you take that same bottle, and only mark it up 1.4 to $112, you may sell 20 bottles. That's 20 x $32 profit = $640. The customers are thrilled with the deal, the servers have made more money in tips, and you've made $320 in profits," smiles Szczesny.

A tip to encourage the purchase of a bottle rather than multiple, single by-the-glass options: Since a five-ounce pour is average around the country for by-the-glass pours and bottles have about 25 ounces per 750 ml bottle, price your by-the-glass offerings at 25% of the bottle price so you encourage folks to order the whole bottle in order to get the fifth glass for free.

"While I love a great glass of wine and have a passion for it, I find myself a simple consumer. There is not much that I do not like... what I dislike, is not finishing the bottle."

CHIP MCMULLIN, EXECUTIVE CHEF,
ST. REGIS DEER VALLEY

PROOFING

CHAPTER FIVE

DOES ANYONE REALLY CARE ABOUT MISTAKES ON MY LIST?

I was working with a pricey chain restaurant. The business development director, Carrie, and I had put a lot of time into the process and had developed a comprehensive list, offering many interesting domestic and international offerings. It was a corporate list so Carrie was using a computer program that autoloaded many of the wines from the wine list-creation company into the draft we were developing. When I got the proof, I noticed typos like "Pino Grigio" and "Chateau Ste. Michele" (supposed to be "Michelle"). There were other wines listed that didn't have an appellation of origin. On one of the entries, the "$" sign was missing.

I emailed Carrie at the restaurant, who emailed her contact at corporate. She was told that this was "just the way it is." I pointed out that it would look like we just didn't care. She said, "I understand that this is the message we are sending, but we can't do anything since it is loaded by corporate."

Setting a pretty low bar, eh? How hard would you have to work to ensure you don't have any typos or mistakes in your wine list? Guess what? Even that little effort would trump an expensive, national chain.

I can tell you that, as a wine drinker, when I look at a wine list like that, I wonder if they are keeping the bottles fresh; I question whether they are being stored at the proper temperature so that they don't degrade; and, I won't enjoy my wine as much as I would if I had confidence in the restaurant.

Pretty harsh for a few typos, but typos show lack of concern and that makes me less confident as a customer. Wine is more than a product in a glass; it is has to be cared for from the vine through bottling into storage and into my glass – my trust for a restaurant like this leaks out of me with each mistake I see.

I can guarantee you that, although I'd probably order a glass of wine from this restaurant, I'm surely not going to put down any real money for a nice bottle since I don't know if they've been taking care of it.

They surely haven't been taking care of their list.

"I hate when I see the house wine is something really lame like some generic grocery store brand. Be creative for crap sake! Take the time to try some cheap wines and pick one that is actually good!"

REBEKAH ABRAMS, OWNER AND EXECUTIVE CHEF AT REBEKAH'S KITCHEN

PRODUCT QUALITY

STEP TWO

"I was out for dinner in New York and I could not decide between two wines so after talking about it with my friend, I ordered one, figuring I'd order the other one next. The server took the order and came back with a small taster of each wine. She said she had heard my debating and took the liberty of letting me taste before she actually brought the wine I ordered. I loved that wonderful customer service."

JODIE ROGERS, EXECUTIVE CHEF AT
DEER VALLEY RESORT

"*While my wife and I were dining at a restaurant along the Riverwalk in San Antonio, the young server brought us a bottle of Cabernet. She very gingerly opened the cork. She explained that opening the bottle too quickly might 'bruise the wine.' Apparently, according to her, the sudden change in atmospheric pressure caused by opening the bottle too quickly would send the wine back in time to when it was just a grape waiting to be fermented, and then would damage it to the point that it was unworthy to be consumed. Our wine made only the slightest 'pop' upon opening. The sound was sufficiently quiet to convince our server that the wine was 'unbruised,' and she began pouring the wine for us.*"

Tom Woodbury, Chef, Cookbook Author

TEMPERATURE

CHAPTER SIX

DOES SERVING TEMPERATURE REALLY MATTER?

Once I ordered a really nice glass of Pinot Noir at a very pricey American contemporary restaurant. My wine came; I swirled and sniffed. Ouch! The nice, light Oregon Pinot filled my sinus cavity with alcohol fumes. Perhaps the wine was off balance... I took a sip. No, not off balance, but the temperature of the wine was somewhere around 75 degrees! No wonder the alcohol was scorching my nostrils.

I asked if the bartender could cool down my wine. (This is challenging to do for a by-the-glass wine, BTW.) She poured the wine into a rocks glass and stuck it in the ice. (Good solution.) I asked her to leave it there for about five minutes, all the while enduring extremely condescending looks. As I waited, I watched where they kept their by-the-glass red wine bottles. They were keeping them on top of one of the low, bar refrigerators at the side of a sink. Basically they were heating them up.

I looked around the restaurant, thinking about all the customers I saw who were drinking red wine by-the-glass, probably not enjoying it as much as they normally do, but just not sure why.

The warmer the liquid the more easily and quickly it evaporates. The enjoyment of wine is not just about drinking the wine, but also enjoying the various aromas. When a wine is too cold, the aromas are stifled. When the wine is too warm, the aromas are overwhelmed by alcohol vapors as they become highly evaporative.

Part of what we go to restaurants for is the aromatic experience. Imagine serving one of your signature dishes with plastic wrap over it. Same as serving your whites too cold. And just as your nose flares when a server puts down a batch of Buffalo wings in front of you, so will your guests' noses sizzle when reds are too hot.

Beverages have optimum temperatures for serving to maximize the enjoyment of them. Imagine serving a warm Coke. Or lukewarm coffee. Wine is no different. It shows well when it is served at its optimum temperature.

An easy way for me to remember the approximate temperature to serve wine is to think of "40-50-60."

- 40 degrees for sparkling
- 50 for whites
- 60 for reds

These are temperature guidelines, not rules. More complex, fuller bodied whites can easily be served at almost 60 degrees. Lighter-bodied, fruity reds can be chilled to 55 degrees and taste great. But in general, if you can aim to serve your wines at the above temperatures, you'll hit the mark for your guests.

TOOLS

CHAPTER SEVEN

WHAT KIND OF GLASSES SHOULD I PROVIDE?

I sat at a cutting edge, pricey restaurant waiting for my glass of wine before dinner. They had a very creative menu, and one that had enticed me to order rabbit (seriously, and I even had a pet bunny named Nibbles when I was 10). I was completely surprised when my Merlot, suggested by Jim, one of the owners, as great with the rabbit, came in a six-ounce glass filled to "almost-spilling-over-the-rim." Since I was just getting to know this restaurateur, I didn't want to object right off the bat, but I was seriously confused. Here was an owner who obviously cared to be creative with his food, and was into wine enough to have tasted his wines with his dishes in order to provide me a great dining experience. And here was my insanely full glass. I lowered my head to the table and carefully brought the glass to my lips.

The experience of wine is upwards of 85% aroma, and if guests can't swirl the wine, you are robbing them of those aromas until they are almost finished with the wine. The alcohol in the wine, along with aroma molecules, becomes airborne, especially when swirled. The aromas come off the wine's surface and they are briefly trapped in the glass by the rounded walls. The wine drinker has the opportunity to smell as he or she sips, which adds tremendously to the enjoyment of the wine.

As I ate, I saw Claire, Jim's wife and co-owner. She came to the table and we chatted. I asked about the glasses. She said that when she had larger glasses, she had complaints from customers that they didn't feel they were getting a full pour because the five ounces of wine didn't look like much in an 18 ounce glass.

Inexperienced wine drinkers, yes, but they have a point. Going to a super small glass, however, isn't the answer.

There are a couple ways to get around this challenge. Use "quartinos," which are glass-sized carafes, to present your by-the-glass (BTG) wines. Your guest sees the full vessel and is satisfied, and your servers can present the wines with a flourish, offering to pour a few ounces into whatever size glass you choose, thus increasing the service experience for the guests.

Or use a large, 18-oz wine glass, and as Mike Szczesny, a Level II Sommelier suggests, have your servers do a bit of educating with your guests each time they present a BTG wine. "We are serving your wine in a large glass so that you can have the enjoyment of the aromas in the glass as the wine opens up. Eighty-five percent of your experience of wine comes through your nose, so we hope you have fun swirling!" Wine and entertainment. Perfect!

In regards to the types of glasses you need, since we are talking about casual to mid-level restaurants, at most you need four types: flutes for sparkling; shorter, smaller-bowled for dessert; and either a white and red glass (or a universal wine glass) that has a 10-ounce capacity at a minimum.

Keep them simple and value priced so you don't need a loan every time you need to restock.

WHAT KIND OF WINE KEYS SHOULD I RECOMMEND TO STAFF?

Double-hinged wine keys are the best. With two leverage points, the cork is not bent to the point of breaking, like it can be with a single-hinged key. They can take a little getting used to, but are compact, have a knife for cutting, and are not super expensive. I carry one made by the Screw-Pull Company called "The Waiter's Friend" which costs about $10, but there are many others that will work. Make sure you ask your wine reps if they have some to share.

WHAT OTHER TOOLS WILL I NEED FOR PROPER WINE SERVICE?

I was teaching a wine tasting 101 class for a group of servers at a steakhouse location in an upscale mall. They were a really friendly group, ribbing each other as the class started. When I teach, I demonstrate how to open a bottle, and then hand out free double-hinged wine keys to the volunteers who come to the front and open subsequent bottles in front of their peers. Southern Wine & Spirits happily foots the bill for these giveaways for restaurants that carry their brands.

One of the newer servers, Janine, broke the cork in the bottle. I tried to get the last piece of cork out, but didn't succeed and it dropped into the wine bottle along with pieces of the broken cork. She was so embarrassed. I looked to the owner, a beautiful, dark-haired woman of about 50 named Suzanne, and asked for a funnel with a filter and a decanter. I was looking forward to this great teaching opportunity.

Unfortunately, Suzanne didn't have any of these tools. I asked what she's done in the past in this situation.

"I take the wine to the back of the house," she explained, "and pour it through a coffee filter into a clean water pitcher to get the pieces out. Then I use a plastic funnel to pour the wine back into the bottle." We all know that some of the pieces of cork would remain in the bottle, but I don't want to call her on this in front of her staff.

"Well, okay," I say, "after the class is over, let's talk about an easier way I have for you."

Suzanne went to lot of work to avoid spending between $23 and $84 on a wine funnel with a filter and a decanter. AND, importantly, the server missed an awesome opportunity to offer additional service to the customers. Even in casual restaurants, a server using tools like the funnel, filter and decanter and "saving" the wine with an elegant pouring at the table is golden, not only to the affected table but to the entire restaurant; customer satisfaction skyrockets and tips go through the roof.

It is important to have the following tools available in your restaurant. Of course, if you are hesitant to allow servers to use some of these tools, at least your manager should know how to use them. This list will be useful for casual to mid-level restaurants.

- Champagne buckets, if you carry sparkling wine (one per five tables).

- White wine chillers (one per five tables – I would only use these when customers ask for them. A properly chilled white wine will be fine sitting on the table for at least a half hour without being in a cold container.).

- Wine funnel with a screen or filter (one is usually plenty).

- Decanters (one per ten tables).

- Double-hinged wine keys for servers to borrow (stock many… ask for them from your wine reps!).

- Cloth napkins to be used when presenting and pouring the wine.

- Plastic wine stoppers or a wine preservation system.

Check out *www.CulinaryWineInstitute.com/resources* for links to suppliers and other ideas that may help you.

These are small pieces of insurance that save wine and can increase customer satisfaction. Plus, you can save your coffee filters for making your coffee.

A story I heard from a confident server named Matt, as he opened a screw cap bottle at my table: "The reason you see so many screw caps nowadays is because cork trees are going extinct. The problem for them is that they have seeds that are germinated in the digestive tract of the Dodo bird, which, as you know, is extinct itself. So since the Dodos are no longer living in Central America, where cork trees grow, wine companies have been starting to go to screw caps since cork is getting so expensive."

KIRSTEN FOX, AUTHOR

STORAGE

CHAPTER EIGHT

WHERE SHOULD I STORE OUR WINES?

There are times when I meet with restaurant managers or owners and the discussion starts with "I don't have much storage space." When that is the issue, we start with figuring out exactly how many bottles, boxes, etc., they have room for in the refrigerator, in the bar and/or in the office under the old desk in the corner. Storing wines properly is key to keeping them from spoiling.

Just like you wouldn't serve limp lettuce to your customers, pouring baked or mishandled wine is a quality problem that will affect your customers' perception of you and your restaurant. The challenge I see over and over is that for non-wine lovers, wine is wine. It doesn't matter whether the wine has been sitting next to a refrigerator – at 75 degrees, vibrating as the fridge is opened and closed and the motor goes on and off – the bottle hasn't been opened and it looks the same so it must be fine.

The problem is that the bottle may not taste the same, kind of like the difference between a home-baked fresh chocolate chip cookie and one you find at the back of your snack cabinet. Both are chocolate chip cookies and they look the same, but the stale one would taste awful.

So because you can't taste each bottle of wine before it's served, you have to take precautions to ensure it has the highest likelihood to get to the table fresh. That means the following three guidelines should be followed as closely as possible…

- Steadily cool storage area (60 degrees max to keep the wines from baking).
- Minimal light (too much ultraviolet light can hasten spoilage).
- Minimize vibration (vibration causes the chemical aging process going on inside the bottle to speed up).

Set up your area the best way possible given the above priorities. Then deliver wine that has been properly stored. You may have to decrease the number of wines you show on your list, but you will be sure that the quality is high and your customers are getting a great experience.

HOW DO WE STORE OPEN BOTTLES, PARTICULARLY REDS?

Behind the bar at a small-town, American-casual restaurant were the five bottles of red wines that the restaurant served by the glass. A couple of them were 750-ml bottles, and three were 1500-ml. All were open and corked with the original cork. I asked Janine, the bar manager who was also a student at a nearby college, how long the bottles had been open.

"We go through a lot of the Cab, Malbec and the Pinot, so those are probably, at the most, a couple days old," she said as she lifted each bottle. *"The Sangiovese and Merlot... I have no idea how old those are."*

Are they stored on the counter all the time, I asked.

"Ummm... yes, why?" was her reply.

Wine is fruit juice and it spoils when it is exposed to oxygen. Just like the spoiling of fruit is delayed when it is chilled, so is the spoiling of wine.

Put open wine bottles in the fridge every night with an impermeable cork, a vacuum sealed plastic cork, or best case, a nitrogen system.

Take reds out of the fridge when the staff shows up for pre-shift work. They'll warm up in time to serve your customers.

In addition, every day a key bartender or manager should pour a small taste of each of the open wines to ensure they are still fresh enough to serve the guests.

SHOULD I CONSIDER POURING OUT OF BOXES?

If you own a very casual restaurant and want to increase profits, one of the first questions to ask yourself is "Why not boxes?"

1. There are some really tasty ones available now.
2. They offer some of the best values (4 bottles/20 glasses of wine are in each box).
3. Because the inner bladder shrinks as the wine is removed, oxygen doesn't get to the wine, so boxes preserve open wine for weeks instead of days.

4. Since both the plastic bladder and the cardboard box are recyclable, they are much better for the environment.

They were invented in Australia by Thomas Angove back in 1965. The original design was a gallon-sized plastic bag held inside a corrugated box. To access the wine, you had to open the lid of the box, cut off a corner of the bag, figure out a way to pour wine out of the opening into a glass, and then fold down the corner of the open bag and clip it shut. Thankfully, Charles Malpas and Penfolds Winery, came up with an air-tight spigot design in 1967.

If you're open to this idea, start with boxed by-the-glass offerings, and, if you need more options, add two or three 750-ml tiers in each varietal category.

Here is an example of the Chardonnay section from a wine list that I just created for a casual, Mexican restaurant in a small mountain town.

- Big House Chardonnay $5 (BTG only and poured from a box).
- Meridian Chardonnay $7/$28 (upsell BTG and low-priced bottle offering).
- La Crema Chardonnay $39 (upsell bottle offering).

Boxes make sense for casual restaurants where diners want tasty wine at a low price.

SERVER TRAINING

STEP THREE

"I teach the same short class twice a week for my front and back of house staff, so they have two opportunities to learn or reinforce the topic. I strive to teach them a new language, how to articulate what they are experiencing as they taste."

SHAWN HYER, GM AND PARTNER AT PARK CITY, UTAH'S SILVER RESTAURANT, AND SOMMELIER II

"*I ordered a young red that I wanted to be a little colder, so I asked the server for an ice bucket so I could drop the bottle temperature a few degrees. Suddenly I got this nonsense wine lecture from her about whites and reds, meats, fish and temperature, that I had to stop by asking her who was paying for the wine?*"

ELIO SCANU, ES CONSULTING R&D

WHO

CHAPTER NINE

SHOULD I TRUST MY WINE REP TO CONDUCT TRAINING?

I walked into a casual, continental cuisine restaurant that had a fun vibe and was busy, even when I was there at 2:30 p.m. I asked to talk to the manager or owner and Kyle, a handsome, 30-something guy, came up and shook my hand.

"Hi Kyle," I said, "Just checking in regarding your wine program. Wanted to hear about your wines, if they're selling, and how you're handling server training."

Kyle nodded like he had everything under control, "Oh, ya, thanks anyway. But, we have a good rep from 'X Distributor' who helps us with our list and training. We don't really need additional help."

"Oh, okay. How often is he able to come in to help you?" I asked, "And what does he cover when he's here?"

Kyle told me that the rep typically visited every three to four weeks and chose topics based on what the rep thought the staff needed to learn.

I asked, "So what happens when you have a new hire?"

Kyle answered, "They just wait until the next time he's at the restaurant."

"Do you keep track of who's at the trainings?" I wondered.

"Not possible," he shook his head. "It is just a pre-service, so whoever is there gets the training."

Using a free system with something as important and potentially profitable as your wine sales training is a mistake for so many reasons:

- The training may only happen three or four times a year.

- The wine rep selects the topics, which may or may not be relevant to what you need.

- The wines covered are probably only the ones that the rep wants your team to sell because they are his products.

- Your servers aren't held accountable for information because you don't know if they were present.

- Given the industry, wine reps change almost as often as servers. What if the next rep isn't a good trainer?

Put something in place that is consistent, reliable and imparts quality information. And hold your servers accountable for that information!

Systems that might work for you:

- On a regular schedule, weekly for example, offer interested servers an extra $20 to prep something to share with the team on a wine from your list.

- Print info sheets on each of your wines and hand them out to your servers. Ask servers to find an interesting story on each and present to the group at pre-service on a weekly basis. Info sheets are posted for a week and then taken down. (Free "Wine Storytime" form at *www.CulinaryWineInstitute.com/storytime*.)

- Use online wine sales training to ensure that all servers understand the basics of wine.

- Hire a local wine educator or sommelier to come into your restaurant on a regular basis, at a minimum monthly.

WILL MY EXISTING STAFF HELP NEW SERVERS UNDERSTAND WINE?

I was at an Asian restaurant working with Eddie on his wine list. He was a young man, sporting a dangling earring. He owned a sushi restaurant in a slightly seedy part of a small town. Despite litter in the gutters around the streets, his restaurant looked clean and inviting. We discussed the small town in which the restaurant was located, and the mix of wines Eddie wanted to offer. After chatting about the wine list, I broached the subject of server wine sales knowledge.

"My team is great," Eddie leaned back in his chair, his earring waggling. "They can sell wine. We do have one new server, but she seems to be picking up everything from my staff really quickly. We don't need any server training."

As I hung out in the restaurant taking pictures of their list, I waited to pick up on any wine discussions. Nothing.

I approached one of the seasoned servers and asked about wine training. He said, with a shrug, "We're kind of on our own here. Luckily most of us drink, so we can figure out how to sell wine."

I asked, "Do you guys help new servers understand your wines with your foods?"

"Ahhh... As far as I know, that's Eddie's job," he said as he grabbed a tray.

Sounds like Eddie's interpretation was based on what he wanted to hear and see, not what was really going on. What did you talk about when you were a server? Probably not the way an off-dry white helps cool the mouth after a spicy food is eaten.

At the very least, on the server's initial training day, if Eddie provided a quick, one hour overview of the wines on the list and how they matched the dishes, the server would have been much better prepared to 1) help guests and 2) sell more wine.

In fact, one of the most helpful documents I've used to train servers is the restaurant's food menu with suggested wines shown after each item. This can hang in the kitchen in an easily accessible area. Better yet, servers can be asked to memorize at least one type of wine that would pair with each dish.

Unless you have a staff of wanna-be wine educators, don't leave the new-hire training to peers. It probably won't happen.

SHOULD I CHARGE MY MANAGER WITH TRAINING MY STAFF?

I worked with one restaurant group that was growing faster than I've ever seen. They had opened three restaurants in two years. Then they got a bad review for one of their restaurants, particularly in regards to the wine service. When I met with the GM of the group and one of his executive chefs, they were humbled and trying to figure out a way to address the problems that the restaurant critic had pointed out.

"Yes, we need regular wine training for our staff," the GM, Jonathan, said. "This kind of review is totally unacceptable and something that we need to get on top of." The chef nodded his head.

We talked about my company's online, proven wine sales training and after outlining the costs, both nodded their heads and said, "We need this."

After that meeting, they began waffling and started avoiding my calls. When I next spoke to Jonathan, he said one of the things I repeatedly hear when I talk to GMs and owners: "We just hired a new manager at one of our restaurants who knows wine really well. He is going to train the staff at all of our restaurants now."

Recognize the limits of one person. Managers at most restaurants are busy enough for three people, without additional wine training duties. Set in place regular, consistent wine training – either provided by someone else who is paid to be at your restaurant, or through online training.

What will work for your restaurant? Ask some of your servers what they've seen work best in other restaurants at which they've worked. Consult with restaurateurs in other parts of the country. I've offered many ideas sprinkled throughout this book, and in fact in the last chapter, I outline my solution for keeping training squarely in focus.

You must put something in place that is consistent so your servers don't end up at your tables in front of a restaurant critic who's just waiting to see a mistake.

"Regular training of servers is almost non-existent in the industry. It can really become a competitive advantage for any owner who decides to actually make an effort and is consistent."

PATRICK DELANEY, 25-YEAR INDUSTRY VETERAN AND DIRECTOR OF PHOENIX DIVISION OF SOUTHERN WINE & SPIRITS

WHAT

CHAPTER TEN

WHAT DOES MY TEAM KNOW?

Most managers and owners have no idea what their staff actually knows about wine. With the constant turnover, lack of consistent wine training and difficulty tracking who is in pre-shift meetings, it's no wonder that no one can figure out where to begin.

I've developed an easy-to-use, 24-question wine test that can help you assess where your team is strong and where your team needs help. Download it at *www.WineProfitPackage.com.*

No matter what path you decide to take following the testing, at least you'll know where your staff needs the most training.

ARE THERE FOOD AND WINE PAIRING MISTAKES TO AVOID?

You're at your cousin's wedding in San Diego, California. Jenny and her now-husband, Clark, picked a destination wedding location instead of their home town of Bakersfield, so you're psyched to be there for them. The wedding ceremony was lovely, right on the bay, and now you're enjoying the reception. In fact, the cake was just cut and a server hands you a piece of chocolate swirl cake with cherry filling and a creamy, white whipped frosting. Yum. You take a few bites and realize that the microphone is on and the speeches are beginning. You grab a flute of Champagne from the nearest server and join the group to hear the best man's thoughts. He is funny and does a good job of reminiscing without bringing up potentially embarrassing stories.

"And so, here's to Jenny and Clark, and may they have many, many years of great times together," the best man raises his glass. You lift yours and take a sip.

Blech!!!! You might as well be drinking straight, carbonated lemon juice. You literally shudder as the acidic Champagne rolls over your taste buds, which were formerly covered in various versions of sugar. The acid after the sweet has completely ruined both the cake and the Champagne. For non-drinkers, think of a glass of fresh lemonade after a chocolate chip cookie.

Many people spend a lot of time analyzing, writing and talking about the best food and wine pairings. You can go into any book store and find many titles by food industry experts suggesting what to do with each type of food, and in fact, how to specifically pair wines with not only the center-of-the-plate item, but each side dish.

More often than not, I've found these to be overkill. The nuances described in some of these books are lost on 95% of the population and the other 5% can probably suggest four other wines that might have worked just as well with their meal.

So I've found that it is often faster and easier to discover pairings *to avoid* rather than to figure out great matches for everything. These bad pairings are the ones that will ruin the meal, not just be a different version of perfect.

So you can choose to cross your fingers and hope that what your servers are suggesting will work, or you can help them become informed so they avoid some very common mistakes.

MISTAKE #1: CHOOSING A HIGHLY ACIDIC WINE TO GO WITH A SWEET DESSERT...

Per the wedding story… tart wine with a sweet can be awful.

The way to fix this is to always suggest a wine that is slightly sweeter than the dessert. At the wedding, a better option would have been a demi-sec sparkling wine. If you have chosen not to offer any sweet dessert wines on your list, teach your staff to suggest your amazing coffee.

MISTAKE #2: RECOMMENDING ONE TYPE OF WINE WITH ALL YOUR DISHES...

This especially happens to wine beginners because, as they start learning about wines, they'll find a wine they actually like and are confident suggesting. That wine can too easily become their go-to idea for everything on your menu.

But no matter what wine they're in love with, it will not enhance all the foods at your restaurant and it will definitely taste awful with some of them. Don't subject your guests to your beginning servers' current, limited view of the wine world.

The fix for this is to expand their views of the wine world. Keep wine in the focus for server training. At least once a week, find a wine to discuss and let your staff taste it. Talk about what style it is and what it might pair with on your menu.

Otherwise, your staff may be dissuading repeat customers without you knowing it.

MISTAKE #3: PAIRING A HIGH ALCOHOL WINE WITH SPICY FOODS...

Spicy, or hot foods are often made with chilies containing capsaicin which, when it comes into contact with mucous membranes in humans, (and all mammals, in fact) causes a burning feeling. High alcohol wines often impart a hot, or burning sensation themselves. The two together lead to a major fire in your mouth.

The fix for this: suggest a very cold, low-alcohol, off-dry or slightly sweet wine with the spicy food. The sugar will help coat the mouth to minimize the burn and the chill of the wine will help to physically cool the mouth. Or suggest a cold, sparkling wine (or, dare I say it… beer!) to refresh the mouth.

MISTAKE #4: SERVING HIGH-IODINE FISH WITH HIGH-IRON RED WINES...

The iron, and the tannin, react to the iodine in the fish and make the fish taste fishier and the wine taste metallic. High iodine fish are typically, but not limited to, cod, haddock, mackerel, and shellfish.

The amount of iron in red wine is affected by how much iron the grapes absorb from the soil, as well as how the grapes are harvested and processed. The resulting amount of iron in the wine differs from varietal to varietal, location to location, and even from plant to plant. Since the outcome of a mouthful of metal is so undesirable, it is safest to avoid pairing iodine-rich fish with potentially iron rich red wines.

The fix for this is to teach your staff to suggest whites with high iodine fish unless you have tried the pairing before and like it.

MISTAKE #5: CHOOSING A HEAVY, RICH WINE TO PAIR WITH A DELICATE DISH... OR VICE VERSA...

One of the biggest mistakes servers make with their pairing suggestions is not considering the weight or body-style of a dish combined with the weight or body-style of the wine. A bad pairing would be a light white, delicate fish with a big, bold, tannic red wine. The wine would overpower the fish. Or consider the opposite: a heavy, Béarnaise-sauce covered steak served with a light-bodied Pinot Grigio. You might think you're drinking water because the wine will be lost with all the bold flavors of the dish.

The best way to remember which wine should be paired with which dish is the saying, "Same Weights = Great Mates." Discover the weight of the center of the plate-offering and look for a wine to complement it. Their body style should match: light with light, medium with medium, heavy with heavy.

I have a free check-holder sized reference chart for your servers at *www.WineProfitPackage.com*. Print it out and give it to them so they can match food and wine at their tables.

Don't allow your servers to present your fabulous food accidentally paired with something that makes it taste horrible. Not good for repeat customers.

WHAT ARE THE BASICS OF PROPER WINE SERVICE?

For Still Wine

- Determine who is host by who ordered the wine.
- Stand to the host's right.
- Repeat the name and vintage of the wine ordered to the host, showing the bottle.
- Remove the wine key, (I love my double-hinged one,) from your apron.
- Use the blade and cut the foil at the top of the neck under the ridge of the top of the bottle. Remove the foil. Close blade.
- Unfold the corkscrew and place the tip into the cork, as close to the center as possible. Screw down into the cork until the entire length is buried.
- Place first lever on top of bottle lip. Grip the lever and the neck of the bottle firmly with your non-dominate hand. Grab the corkscrew handle and raise it slowly.
- When the first lever can't lift the cork any longer, readjust to the second lever on the bottle lip and continue slowly until the cork gently hisses free.

- Unscrew the cork from the corkscrew and place it to the host's right, on the table.

For Sparkling Wine

- Bring a champagne bucket or stand to the table and place it slightly away from the table.
- Stand to the host's right.
- Repeat the name and vintage of the wine ordered to the host, showing the bottle.
- Remove your wine key and use the blade to cut the foil under the cage at the top of the neck. Close blade, and remove the foil. Place in your apron.
- Put a serving napkin over the bottle, put your thumb over the cork, and untwist the cage, wiggling it after six turns to expand it. (The cork can fly off a bottle at 60 miles per hour so the most important thing to teach your staff is to keep a thumb on top of an unopened sparkling wine cork.)
- Grip the entire cage, cork and napkin, never letting go of the cork, and turn the bottom of the bottle slowly, allowing the cork to gently hiss free.
- Place the entire cork and cage to the right of the host on the table.

Pouring the taste

Wipe the lip of the bottle with a napkin and pour a small sample for the host, about one ounce or so.

If the host nods or accepts the bottle:

Pour around the table, starting with the ladies, then gentlemen, and ending with the host, whether male or female. Wipe the lip of the bottle between pours to minimize drips. Don't touch any of the glasses with the bottle itself; stay an inch or two above the rim of the glass.

A bottle has about 25 ounces. An average table of four would get an initial three to four ounces per glass. Divide the number of wine drinkers into 25 to figure out the MAX number of ounces to pour each person.

Place the bottle on the table to the right of the host with the label facing him or her.

If the host does not accept the bottle...

... because the host says the wine is bad/tainted/ corked/oxidized.

If the wine is tainted, it is usually corked, (a musty smell like a dank basement), or oxidized, (a rich, over-ripe odor best learned by smelling Sherry, or cooking Sherry). If the guest smells something wrong, immediately remove the bottle and glass. Retrieve another bottle and glass and repeat the tasting process.

... because the host does not like the wine.

Sometimes a guest just does not like the wine being poured. Nothing is wrong with the wine; it is just not what the guest wants to drink. Most restaurants I work with ask servers to alert a manager if someone has rejected wine based on preference. The manager talks to the guest, getting more information, and then is responsible to present the next bottle.

Make sure your team is aware of how you want them to handle this situation because a guest with a power issue can run a server ragged opening wines just for the fun of it.

One of my friends related a story to me about this very situation. He was at a very nice resort in Mexico and was with a pompous wine connoisseur who was the host. The server brought a bottle of over-$100 wine to the table – the host rejected it because he did not like the cork. He never tasted the wine. He rejected the next three bottles, as well, because apparently their corks were unacceptable. Finally the sever called the manager in and the host backed down. My friend was mortified to be a part of this experience, but with the proper training and earlier manager involvement, most of it could have been averted.

IS DECANTING REALLY NECESSARY?

It seems a bit formal to discuss decanting for casual to mid-level restaurants, but there are three reasons that it would be appropriate to provide this service no matter what level of restaurant you own: 1) to aerate young, full-bodied reds at the guest's request; 2) to separate the wine from sediment in the bottle; and 3) to appease a customer who wants to impress you or their guests. The first two are technically important, with the third being an opportunity to show service.

One way or another, your servers, or at least your manager, should know how to decant a wine.

For aeration and as a show of service

Young bold reds can use some oxygen in them to soften the sometimes-harsh tannins. If you splash the wine into a flat-bottomed decanter, you introduce as much oxygen as possible into the wine. The reds that do well with this kind of decanting are young Cabernet Sauvignon, Bordeaux, Syrah/Shiraz, Petite Syrah, Nebbiolo, Barolo, and Barbaresco.

The wine bottle is opened as usual at the right of the host, the cork is presented, and then the wine is decanted. The tasting pour is done from the decanter.

For sediment

This kind of decanting is used for either old bottles of red (over 10-15 years) or vintage Port. Minimizing the movement of the liquid in the bottle is paramount because shaking will stir up the sediment.

Pour the wine slowly into a decanter topped with a funnel and screen, leaving about three ounces in the bottle. Some restaurants may use a candle behind the neck of the bottle to watch for sediment coming down, but this is not typical at most casual to mid-level restaurants.

Pour the taste from the decanter. Ask the host if he or she would like the original bottle left on the table or removed with the last few ounces and sediment.

HOW DO SERVERS DEAL WITH BROKEN CORKS?

If a server breaks a cork, it is sometimes successful to try to insert a corkscrew into the remaining piece at a slight angle. If this works, the server should slowly withdraw the piece.

If that doesn't work, often the cork and other small pieces fall into the bottle. If this happens, the server has two options.

Table service save: The server should let the host know of the problem, leave the wine bottle on the table and retrieve a decanter, wine funnel and screen. The server pours the wine into the decanter through the funnel and screen, and pours a taste of wine from the decanter. The server would ask the host if he or she would like the wine bottle left on the table.

Back-of-house save: The server lets the host know of the problem and takes the wine to the back of house. A cork catcher or retriever is used to pull the cork out. The server returns to the table and pours the taste.

"I went into one casual pizzeria that had a 12-bottle list of totally obscure wines. This was in a small county, I mean small. They had a Piquepoul white from France on the list by the glass, but not a Chardonnay. That restaurant owner will never know how many sales were lost because the list was not matched to the area."

MIKE SZCZSNEY, SOMMELIER II AND SALES MANAGER FOR YOUNG'S MARKET

WHEN

CHAPTER ELEVEN

WHEN IS THE BEST TIME FOR SERVER TRAINING?

Make sure new hires are trained before they get on the floor in front of your guests. With server turnover conservatively estimated at 50% per year, consistent wine training should be set up and ready to go immediately.

In regards to ongoing training, getting the team together is a challenge, especially if your restaurant is open throughout the day. I have done training at 9:30 p.m. on a Monday and 8:00 a.m. on a Sunday because the managers and owners at these restaurants were committed to training their staff. These times are challenging to implement long-term, but they may be your only option.

At the very least, highlight wine at least once per week at the pre-shift meeting.

Just pick a low-impact time for your restaurant and make it happen on a regular basis.

"If you want great staff, you must care about them, like family. You need to learn to give and be understanding. When you treat them well and give them great training, they stay with you, so you have a great core team. I am confident in them and they know it."

HANS FUEGI, OWNER OF MANY RESTAURANTS OVER 30 YEARS INCLUDING GRUB STEAK RESTAURANT IN PARK CITY, UTAH

WHERE

CHAPTER TWELVE

WHERE SHOULD I HOLD MY STAFF MEETINGS?

Anywhere that you can have the team together, preferably where they can also taste the wine that is being discussed. That can be in your restaurant area, the bar, the kitchen, or the back dock. It doesn't need to be fancy.

Aside from tasting the wine as it's being discussed, if possible, there is one key ingredient for a successful wine training: the team must be able to hear you or whoever is speaking. If you are in an area that is loud due to kitchen equipment or outside noise, I'd suggest you buy a mini, portable microphone and speaker. I bought one for $35 called a Pyle Pro PWMA50B Public Address System. It simply has a microphone on a headband with a cord that attaches to a very small, battery-operated speaker on your belt.

Just getting the team together somewhere, anywhere to talk about wine at least once a week will increase your wine sales.

"Way too often, the server's answer to my question of 'Which wine would you recommend?' is, 'Do you prefer red or white?' ARRGHH! When someone starts off by wanting to compartmentalize your question into two large (and totally irrelevant) categories says that they either know NOTHING about wine or they assume that YOU KNOW NOTHING about wine. Smarter and less insulting questions would be: What are your dinner choices this evening? Are you celebrating something special this evening? Which kinds (or varietals) of wine do you usually enjoy? Do you prefer something fruity, light, or more robust?"

AMATO DE CIVITA, PRESIDENT AND OWNER OF WINE AWAKENINGS

WHY

CHAPTER THIRTEEN

SHOULD MY SERVERS ASSIST CUSTOMERS WITH WINE CHOICES?

Jessica, a slightly plump, blonde woman in her twenties, came over to greet me after I had asked to see the manager. The restaurant was a small, casually classic place in an historic section of a small city – a lot of brick, brass and wood. Handing her my wine rep card, I asked how her wine list was working or if she needed any help with training.

"Our customers understand wines," she explained, *"so our servers don't really need a lot of training. If our servers started talking about wine with our customers, it may insult them."*

Informed servers helping guests would insult them? Interesting, I thought to myself.

Looking at the wine list, I asked, "Are all the wines selling pretty well?"

"Well, out of the wines on the list," she answered, *"we really sell the California wines almost exclusively. And a few Australian ones."*

"I see an Albariño on the list here," I pointed out. *"How is this one selling."*

"Oh, it doesn't sell at all," she snorted, "because our customers only like California wines. Not sure why the owner even has that on there."

"What would your servers say if someone asked about it?" I queried.

"They wouldn't really have anything to say," she said with a titch of sass, "because no one asks about them."

Assuming customers know wine because they aren't asking questions is leaving money on the table. Just like customers expect your team to do a good job of explaining what food is available at your restaurant, you will make a lot more money if they do a good job explaining the wine available at your restaurant.

And suggesting options that trigger customers to consider something out of their normal routine will increase sales:

- May I start you off with something bubbly tonight? (Sets the stage for a special night.)
- Have you made a wine selection this evening?
- Are you interested in a wine to go with your first course?
- I just learned an interesting story about...
- Are you in the mood for...
- Would you be interested in a suggestion for a wine with your entrée?
- We just tried the _____ with our special. It pairs beautifully because X, Y and Z highlight the dish's flavors.

- If you like "X-common-wine," you may want to try the "Y-less-common-wine," which is similar yet will offer a different twist of flavor and aroma.

Of course, some states have restrictions on using these kinds of questions, but after following the law, your servers should ask leading questions.

If the guests just wanted to place an order for food, they could have taken it "to go." Because your restaurant and your team offers them a dining experience – food and drink, atmosphere and enjoyment – make sure your team is adequately prepared to speak about anything on both your food menu and your beverage list.

"What I've seen happen so many times… the server thinks he knows everything and tells the customer 'Oh sure, I will get you our best Sauvignon Blanc,' and then he brings a red wine."

MARLENE NODA, CHEF AND RESTAURANT MANAGER

"I went to a restaurant and ordered the same ol' wine I always do, mostly because I knew it was safe and I wouldn't waste my money on something I might not enjoy. The server asked if I'd like to try a wine that she'd suggest based on my food order. I was game and loved it. I tipped extra because she had been a part of a great, new experience."

STACY DYMALSKI, AUTHOR, PUBLISHING COACH AND FOODIE

HOW

CHAPTER FOURTEEN

WILL A WINE REFERENCE BOOK HELP TRAIN SERVERS?

At one nice steakhouse, I met with a highly motivated general manager, Carl. He was really interested in helping the servers understand wine and had a pretty good wine knowledge himself. He was a chef and knew that "knowledge is power."

I asked him what he was currently doing to help his staff sell wine. He went into the kitchen and brought out his extremely gorgeous, pristine, three-ring notebook filled with info sheets on each of the wines on his list.

"Wow," I said, "this took a lot of time. How do the servers use this?"

"I keep it right inside the manager's office in the recipe book shelves," he said. "Easy to find and always available."

"How old is this," I asked.

He looked up at the ceiling, "About ten months, let's see, yes, ten months because I had been here about a month," he recalled. "And I update the sheets when we get new wines." There wasn't one spatter of food on the notebook and the paper looked perfect.

Sadly for him and the amount of work he'd put into this notebook, I wondered if any of his servers had ever touched it.

You have to make wine a priority, figuring out a way to incorporate continuous server education into the normal, day-to-day operation of the business. Wine has to be discussed regularly for your staff to feel comfortable about it. Sticking a notebook in the restaurant office as a learning tool is wishful thinking and doesn't work to help your staff.

And furthermore, the sad fact is that most of the sales sheets on wines have little "sellable" information, like stories about the winery or winemaker, or special history that brings the wine to life.

An alternative to a notebook, single info sheets can work to help your servers, IF they are posted in an area where they are easily readable, and IF someone has presented the wine to them in person. The info sheets are a great tool for back up, but not good as the primary means of teaching.

As a primary, ongoing education program, create a program like "$20 Tuesday" or "$50 Friday" depending on the type of restaurant you own. Ask for a volunteer server each week and hand over an info sheet on one of your restaurant's wines. The server has a week to find out interesting facts about it. What are great stories about the wine? What is the most unusual fact the server found? What does the wine go with on the menu and why? Then on the following Tuesday or Friday, the server comes prepared to talk about the wine. After highlighting the wine at the pre-shift meeting, if he or she has done a good job, you personally hand a $20 or $50 bill to him or her in front of the team. You'll be surprised at how quickly your staff will become engaged after seeing that exchange. (See "Wine Storytime" form at *www.CulinaryWineInstitute.com/storytime*.)

HOW SHOULD MY SERVERS TALK ABOUT WINE?

Here is the actual copy from the Cono Sur website about their Chardonnay. *"This Chardonnay is a bright yellow with hints of gold. Its nose displays aromas of white peaches with fruity and citric notes. Complex fruity flavors and minerality create a beautifully balanced palate. This young and fresh wine is perfect for serving with fish, white meats, creams, cheeses and spices, particularly pepper, garlic and chives."*

Cover up the paragraph above with your hand. Repeat three things from the list. Okay, never mind, just try to give me one.

Now consider what would help sell wine, not just describe it. After looking deeper into the Cono Sur website, I came up with this:

Cono Sur Chardonnay is an interesting white wine from the central part of Chile. In 2007, they became the first winery in the world to obtain carbon neutral status. They are committed to organic farming where possible and integrated farming (minimizing chemical usage) at a minimum. The wines are fresh, intense and well-balanced. But they don't take themselves too seriously with the motto: No family trees, no dusty bottles, just quality wine. This is an unoaked wine with aromas of citrus, apple and pear and it goes really well with light dishes like fish, white meats, creams, cheeses and spices, particularly pepper, garlic and chives.

Stories sell wine. Descriptions are merely supporting words. Customers are looking to connect with a wine, feel something when they are drinking it. The more a server can convey about the wine in a great story, the more likely the guests will enjoy the wine.

Most memorable stories center on the people involved in producing the wine. In the example above, even though the story about Cono Sur above doesn't focus on a specific person, it talks about the company's philosophy about conserving the environment, which is a very human, personal issue.

Find stories about your wines to help your servers make them connect to your guests.

IS THERE AN EXAMPLE OF AN IDEAL SERVER-TRAINING PROGRAM?

The ongoing system I recommend is one I designed specifically to help independent restaurateurs take control of their server training.

1. Start new hires with a basic wine test to determine what kind of wine sales knowledge they have. (Wine tests available at *www.WineProfitPackage.com.*)

2. If servers don't pass the test, put them into an online wine sales training program to give

them the basics BEFORE they are on the floor helping customers. Online training works for a variety of reasons:

- Servers do the training at their convenience.

- Servers are tested so you're ensured they are learning.

- It is less expensive than live training.

- Every person gets consistent, clear information and you can hold them accountable for what they've learned.

- You see certificates from those servers who have been a part of wine sales training so you don't have to keep track of who knows what.

(Restaurant bulk pricing and information at *www.CulinaryWineInstitute.com*.)

3. Create a server wine engagement incentive called "$20 Tuesdays" or "$50 Fridays." Each week, one server is given one wine from your list to study, trying to find interesting stories about the wine, and good pairings from your menu. The server presents the information about the wine and the wine is tasted at the following Tuesday or Friday pre-shift meeting. (Free "Wine Storytime" form at *www.CulinaryWineInstitute.com/storytime*.)

4.   Once a week or month depending on your
staff's experience, at a pre-shift meeting, your
manager calls a server up to demonstrate one
aspect of table service.
(Free "Tableside Tune Up" ideas at
www.CulinaryWineInstitute.com/tuneup.)

5.   As the team's skills increase and if your
restaurant calls for higher levels of service and
knowledge, use additional wine sales training
levels available online. (See additional levels
available at *www.CulinaryWineInstitute.com*.)
Reward advanced study with something
valuable to your servers. I've seen iTunes gift
cards, bottles of great wine, complementary
dinners at your restaurant, concert tickets,
hotel stays, etc.

*"Can't stand it when I walk into a restaurant
and the list is the exact same as it is at the next
restaurant. And the next. And so on. Very safe
and very, very boring."*

JASON JENSEN, SEASONED CULINARY PRO

CONCLUSION

If you saw yourself in any of the stories I've included, you're not alone. The fact that you've read this book and are making an effort to take control of your wine program will be a huge differentiating feature of your restaurant versus your competitors.

As an interesting side note, I have seen the quality of employees at restaurants committed to their wine programs go up substantially after the owners or managers start focusing on them. As the local population of restaurant employees begins to notice the emphasis you're putting on training them, top managers in the area will want to come work for you.

As these quality-driven managers join your team, the servers they manage will need to either perform or be nudged out. Your reputation in the area will increase and your restaurant will become a place at which servers want to work, feel rewarded and valued, and they will stay longer with you, decreasing your turnover and, with that, so many problems.

This is the first edition of *The Profitable Wine List*. I am hopeful that, as it is used around the country, you will share your stories of before and after, things that went wrong and changed for the better. Email me at *kfox@CulinaryWineInstitute.com*.

We also have a Facebook page for our company at *www.Facebook.com/CulinaryWineInstitute*, and a Facebook group for those interested in being a part of our wine in restaurants conversation at *www.Facebook.com/TheProfitableWineList*.

And, you can follow my blog at *www.CulinaryWineInstitute.com/blog*.

I can also be found on Twitter at *@kirstenfox_wine*.

Good luck with your wine list and I hope I hear great stories from you as you squeeze more profitability out of this part of your restaurant world.

ACKNOWLEDGEMENTS

Preparation for this book started in 2004 when Sara Henry, my sister, allowed me to teach wine tasting classes at her Park City, Utah, wine accessory store, The Art of Wine. I fell in love with the subject and began to search out ways to be more involved.

As I developed businesses focused on wine education, I was guided by coaches, mentors, and advocates particularly Bill Brown, Roi Agneta and Ron Baron, who were a part of an organization called Entrepreneurial Launch Pad.

Mike Szczesny, one of my first professors at Fox School of Wine, showed me how powerful a sense of humor can be in regards to wine. And Dave Engen, Vice President of Young's Market Mountain States Division, saw my vision and supported me early in the development of Culinary Wine Institute.

Hans Fuegi, owner of Grub Steak Restaurant and Utah restaurant-industry leader, was my first customer at Culinary Wine Institute. His unwavering support has been critical to keeping my confidence strong through the ups and downs of the last few years.

I was lucky enough to have been hired by Patrick Delaney as a sales rep for his small wine brokerage company, Phoenix Wine & Spirits. His years in the business helped give me the foundation I needed to fuel my growing passion for the restaurant industry. In 2013, his company was purchased by Southern Wine & Spirits.

Tim Taylor, a fellow rep with Phoenix Wine & Spirits and now Southern, has been in the industry for almost 30 years and his assistance and advice were key as I learned new approaches to creating successful wine lists.

Southern Wine & Spirits provided the support, tools and freedom to work in my own way with my client restaurants. Chris DePersio, a national trainer for Southern, offered his national perspective on the book, helping to pull the lens out so all areas of the country would benefit.

After finishing the first draft of my book, George Larson, a friend, suggested I send it to Michela Larson, his sister, who owns many restaurants in the Boston and Florida area to ask for her opinion of the book. She was kind, but gave me the honest feedback that she didn't like the approach I had used. Her input helped me see the book in a different light and re-write it in the format you are reading now.

Local restaurant-industry veteran, David Ringelberg, gave me his insights on the book, as did Rachael Pack, a budding culinary wine student. And Keltin Barney was key in editing the book so it flowed more smoothly. I also used and highly recommend Kevin Rogers and the copy writing team at *www.CopyChief.com* for ways to dial in marketing messages.

As I was on a budget that hardly allowed for anything outside my own hard work, I appreciate that Katie Mullaly offered to design the inside contents. Her excitement to get the book published helped propel me along during the last phases.

And most importantly, I would not have gotten this book published without Stacy Dymalski, author of *The Memoir Midwife: Nine Steps to Self-Publishing Your Book*, my long-time friend and my unexpected peer mentor. From our meetings over tea at Atticus on Main Street in Park City, to her no-nonsense support as I dealt with a breast cancer diagnosis, to her own inspirational devotion to success, I couldn't have done this without her.

Finally, thanks to all the independent restaurant owners who care so much about their customers. So many of my most memorable life experiences center around a table at your establishments. Your hard work and employees create the backdrop for human connection and joy and I appreciate it.

About the Author

Kirsten Henry Fox lives in Park City, Utah, with her husband and the youngest of her three children, along with their yellow lab, and two tabby cats.

Contact Kirsten at *kfox@culinarywineinstitute.com*, or 435-655-WINE (9463), or *@kirstenfox_wine* on Twitter.

NOTES

NOTES

NOTES

NOTES

NOTES

NOTES

NOTES

NOTES

NOTES

NOTES

Made in the USA
Middletown, DE
24 April 2015